Table of Contents

Day: Month: Year:

Conditions:

What:
Where: Time:
Notes:

What:
Where: Time:
Notes:

What:
Where: Time:
Notes:

Day: Month: Year:

Conditions:

What:
Where: Time:
Notes:

What:
Where: Time:
Notes:

What:
Where: Time:
Notes:

Day: Month: Year:

Conditions:

What:
Where: Time:
Notes:

What:
Where: Time:
Notes:

What:
Where: Time:
Notes:

Day: Month: Year:

Conditions:

What:
Where: Time:
Notes:

What:
Where: Time:
Notes:

What:
Where: Time:
Notes:

Day: Month: Year:

Conditions:

What:
Where: Time:
Notes:

What:
Where: Time:
Notes:

What:
Where: Time:
Notes:

Day: Month: Year:

Conditions:

What:
Where: Time:
Notes:

What:
Where: Time:
Notes:

What:
Where: Time:
Notes:

Day: Month: Year:

Conditions:

What:
Where: Time:
Notes:

What:
Where: Time:
Notes:

What:
Where: Time:
Notes:

Day: Month: Year:

Conditions:

What:
Where: Time:
Notes:

What:
Where: Time:
Notes:

What:
Where: Time:
Notes:

Day: Month: Year:

Conditions:

What:
Where: Time:
Notes:

What:
Where: Time:
Notes:

What:
Where: Time:
Notes:

Day: Month: Year:

Conditions:

What:
Where: Time:
Notes:

What:
Where: Time:
Notes:

What:
Where: Time:
Notes:

Day: Month: Year:

Conditions:

What:
Where: Time:
Notes:

What:
Where: Time:
Notes:

What:
Where: Time:
Notes:

Day: Month: Year:

Conditions:

What:
Where: Time:
Notes:

What:
Where: Time:
Notes:

What:
Where: Time:
Notes:

Day: Month: Year:

Conditions:

What:
Where: Time:
Notes:

What:
Where: Time:
Notes:

What:
Where: Time:
Notes:

Day: Month: Year:

Conditions:

What:
Where: Time:
Notes:

What:
Where: Time:
Notes:

What:
Where: Time:
Notes:

Day: Month: Year:

Conditions:

What:
Where: Time:
Notes:

What:
Where: Time:
Notes:

What:
Where: Time:
Notes:

Day: Month: Year:

Conditions:

What:
Where: Time:
Notes:

What:
Where: Time:
Notes:

What:
Where: Time:
Notes:

Day: Month: Year:

Conditions:

What:
Where: Time:
Notes:

What:
Where: Time:
Notes:

What:
Where: Time:
Notes:

Day: Month: Year:

Conditions:

What:
Where: Time:
Notes:

What:
Where: Time:
Notes:

What:
Where: Time:
Notes:

Day: Month: Year:

Conditions:

What:
Where: Time:
Notes:

What:
Where: Time:
Notes:

What:
Where: Time:
Notes:

Day: Month: Year:

Conditions:

What:
Where: Time:
Notes:

What:
Where: Time:
Notes:

What:
Where: Time:
Notes:

Day: Month: Year:

Conditions:

What:
Where: Time:
Notes:

What:
Where: Time:
Notes:

What:
Where: Time:
Notes:

Day: Month: Year:

Conditions:

What:
Where: Time:
Notes:

What:
Where: Time:
Notes:

What:
Where: Time:
Notes:

Day: Month: Year:

Conditions:

What:
Where: Time:
Notes:

What:
Where: Time:
Notes:

What:
Where: Time:
Notes:

Day: Month: Year:

Conditions:

What:
Where: Time:
Notes:

What:
Where: Time:
Notes:

What:
Where: Time:
Notes:

Day: Month: Year:

Conditions:

What:
Where: Time:
Notes:

What:
Where: Time:
Notes:

What:
Where: Time:
Notes:

Day: Month: Year:

Conditions:

What:
Where: Time:
Notes:

What:
Where: Time:
Notes:

What:
Where: Time:
Notes:

Day: Month: Year:

Conditions:

What:
Where: Time:
Notes:

What:
Where: Time:
Notes:

What:
Where: Time:
Notes:

Day: Month: Year:

Conditions:

What:
Where: Time:
Notes:

What:
Where: Time:
Notes:

What:
Where: Time:
Notes:

Day: Month: Year:

Conditions:

What:
Where: Time:
Notes:

What:
Where: Time:
Notes:

What:
Where: Time:
Notes:

Day: Month: Year:

Conditions:

What:
Where: Time:
Notes:

What:
Where: Time:
Notes:

What:
Where: Time:
Notes:

Day: Month: Year:

Conditions:

What:
Where: Time:
Notes:

What:
Where: Time:
Notes:

What:
Where: Time:
Notes:

Day: Month: Year:

Conditions:

What:
Where: Time:
Notes:

What:
Where: Time:
Notes:

What:
Where: Time:
Notes:

Day: Month: Year:

Conditions:

What:
Where: Time:
Notes:

What:
Where: Time:
Notes:

What:
Where: Time:
Notes:

Day: Month: Year:

Conditions:

What:
Where: Time:
Notes:

What:
Where: Time:
Notes:

What:
Where: Time:
Notes:

Day: Month: Year:

Conditions:

What:
Where: Time:
Notes:

What:
Where: Time:
Notes:

What:
Where: Time:
Notes:

Day: Month: Year:

Conditions:

What:
Where: Time:
Notes:

What:
Where: Time:
Notes:

What:
Where: Time:
Notes:

Day: Month: Year:

Conditions:

What:
Where: Time:
Notes:

What:
Where: Time:
Notes:

What:
Where: Time:
Notes:

Day: Month: Year:

Conditions:

What:
Where: Time:
Notes:

What:
Where: Time:
Notes:

What:
Where: Time:
Notes:

Day: Month: Year:

Conditions:

What:
Where: Time:
Notes:

What:
Where: Time:
Notes:

What:
Where: Time:
Notes:

Day: Month: Year:

Conditions:

What:
Where: Time:
Notes:

What:
Where: Time:
Notes:

What:
Where: Time:
Notes:

Day: Month: Year:

Conditions:

What:
Where: Time:
Notes:

What:
Where: Time:
Notes:

What:
Where: Time:
Notes:

Day: Month: Year:

Conditions:

What:
Where: Time:
Notes:

What:
Where: Time:
Notes:

What:
Where: Time:
Notes:

Day: Month: Year:

Conditions:

What:
Where: Time:
Notes:

What:
Where: Time:
Notes:

What:
Where: Time:
Notes:

Day: Month: Year:

Conditions:

What:
Where: Time:
Notes:

What:
Where: Time:
Notes:

What:
Where: Time:
Notes:

Day: Month: Year:

Conditions:

What:
Where: Time:
Notes:

What:
Where: Time:
Notes:

What:
Where: Time:
Notes:

Day: Month: Year:

Conditions:

What:
Where: Time:
Notes:

What:
Where: Time:
Notes:

What:
Where: Time:
Notes:

Day: Month: Year:

Conditions:

What:
Where: Time:
Notes:

What:
Where: Time:
Notes:

What:
Where: Time:
Notes:

Day: Month: Year:

Conditions:

What:
Where: Time:
Notes:

What:
Where: Time:
Notes:

What:
Where: Time:
Notes:

Day: Month: Year:

Conditions:

What:
Where: Time:
Notes:

What:
Where: Time:
Notes:

What:
Where: Time:
Notes:

Day: Month: Year:

Conditions:

What:
Where: Time:
Notes:

What:
Where: Time:
Notes:

What:
Where: Time:
Notes: